Progressive

DRUM GROOVES

by

Craig Lauritsen

Visit our Website
www.learntoplaymusic.com

The Progressive Series of Music Instruction Books, CDs, and DVDs

CD TRACK LISTING

1	[Rock] Ex 1, 3, 5, 7, 9, 11, 13	15	[Rap] Ex 174, 175, 177, 179
2	[Rock] Ex 15, 17, 19, 21, 23, 25, 27	16	[Go-Go/Hip Hop] Ex 181, 183, 185, 187, 189, 191, 193
3	[Rock] Ex 29, 31, 33, 35, 36, 38, 40	17	[Go-Go/Hip Hop] Ex 195, 197, 199, 201, 203, 205, 207
4	[Rock] Ex 41, 43, 45, 46, 50, 51	18	[Funk/Fusion] Ex 209, 211, 213, 215, 217, 219, 221
5	[Rock] Ex 53, 55	19	[Funk/Fusion] Ex 223, 225, 227, 229, 231, 233
6	[Shuffle & Blues] Ex 56, 58, 60, 62, 64, 66, 68	20	[Latin] Ex 235, 237, 238, 240, 241, 242, 244
7	[Shuffle & Blues] Ex 70, 72, 73, 75, 76, 78, 80	21	[Latin] Ex 245, 247, 248, 250, 251, 252, 253
8	[Shuffle & Blues] Ex 82, 84, 86, 87, 89	22	[Latin] Ex 254, 256, 257, 258
9	[Heavy Metal] Ex 91, 93, 96, 99, 101, 104, 106	23	[Swing] Ex 259, 261, 263, 265, 267, 269, 270
10	[Heavy Metal] Ex 108, 110, 112, 114, 116, 118, 120	24	[Swing] Ex 272, 274, 276, 278, 279, 280, 281
11	[Reggae] Ex 121, 123, 125, 127, 130, 132, 134	25	[Swing] Ex 282, 284
12	[Reggae] Ex 136, 139, 141, 143, 144	26	[Odd Time] Ex 285, 287, 289, 290, 292, 294, 295
13	[Rap] Ex 146, 148, 150, 152, 154, 156, 158	27	[Odd Time] Ex 296, 297, 299, 300, 302, 303, 304
14	[Rap] Ex 160, 162, 164, 166, 168, 170, 172	28	[Odd Time] Ex 305, 306, 307, 308

PROGRESSIVE DRUM GROOVES
I.S.B.N. 978 1 875726 31 8
Order Code: CP-72631

Acknowledgments
Photographs: Phil Martin

For more information on this series contact;
L.T.P. Publishing Pty Ltd
email: info@learntoplaymusic.com
or visit our website;
www.learntoplaymusic.com

Published by
KOALA MUSIC
PUBLICATIONS

Contents

Introduction

The boundaries and parameters of music are continually changing and expanding. All drummers, regardless of their specialist style, now need a sound understanding of other styles to keep up with these continual stylistic expansions.

Having a knowledge of many musical styles also allows you to be more creative. This book therefore, is an invaluable aid to drummers, covering 10 of the most popular drumming styles and giving examples of over 300 beats and 130 fills. The book is designed to introduce the drummer to a broad range of styles, techniques and ideas, by showing examples of what can be played in particular musical situations. A knowledge of basic drumming fundamentals is assumed (see *Progressive Drum Method* by Craig Lauritsen).

This book is also a valuable reference guide for anyone interested in drum machine programming.

Examples range in difficulty from relatively simple to very advanced.

All material has been chosen to be interesting and usable with fills being added to certain beats, generally at the end of a 4 or 8 bar passage.

The book has been divided into 10 sections, each covering a particular musical style. Each section has examples listed in a carefully graded progressive format.

Here are a few ideas which are important:

- Play each example twenty times before progressing.

- Experiment with your own ideas as much as possible.

- Try to maintain a positive attitude. Anything is achievable.

- Be patient. Learning is a life long process and should not be limited to a specific period of time.

- Try playing different fills with different beats.

- Try to bring something of yourself into every musical situation.

- HAVE FUN - because that's really what it's all about!

Explanation of Notation

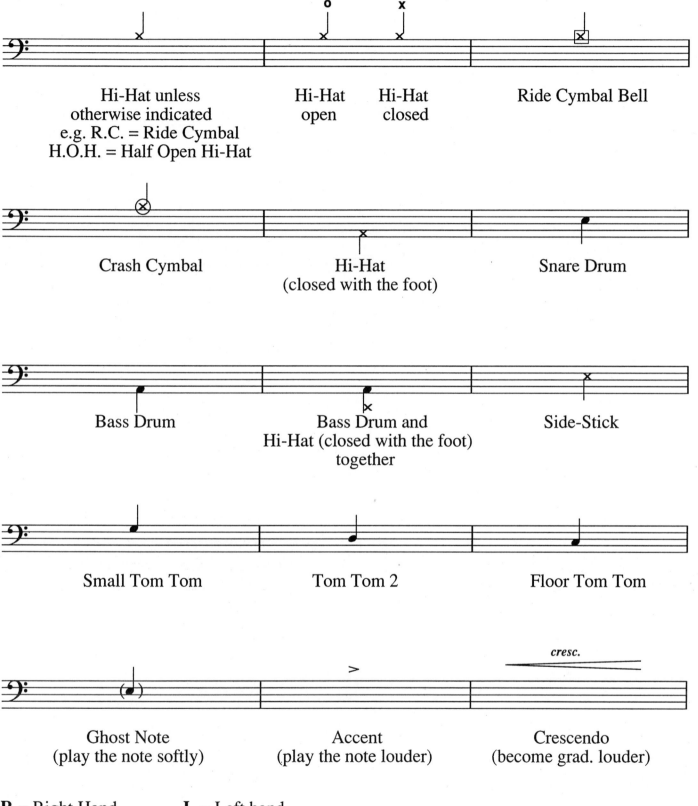

Hi-Hat unless
otherwise indicated
e.g. R.C. = Ride Cymbal
H.O.H. = Half Open Hi-Hat

Hi-Hat
open

Hi-Hat
closed

Ride Cymbal Bell

Crash Cymbal

Hi-Hat
(closed with the foot)

Snare Drum

Bass Drum

Bass Drum and
Hi-Hat (closed with the foot)
together

Side-Stick

Small Tom Tom

Tom Tom 2

Floor Tom Tom

Ghost Note
(play the note softly)

Accent
(play the note louder)

Crescendo
(become grad. louder)

R = Right Hand   **L** = Left hand

A tie with a dotted line indicates that the first beat of the first bar is played the first time through a repeated section. Upon each subsequent repeat the standard tie rule applies.

Note: Unless otherwise indicated, sticking of fills is presumed starting with the right hand and then alternating eg, R L R L etc.

Repeat Signs

There are four symbols in common usage which indicate that a portion of music be repeated.

1) Two dots placed before a double bar line indicate that the music is to be repeated, from the beginning of the piece of music or from a previous set of repeat signs.

Repeat Sign

2) A diagonal line with a dot either side, indicates that the previous bar only is to be repeated.

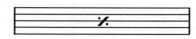

3) The number 2 placed over a bar line crossed with two dotted diagonal lines, indicates that the previous two bars are to be repeated.

4) Diagonal lines are used to indicate that a $^{1}/_{4}$ note length (1 beat) of information per diagonal line, be repeated from the same position of the previous bar, e.g.

SECTION 1
Rock

Rock is a broad category which draws influence from many other styles and hence is continually expanding. General features of the Rock style are:

1) Simple Chords
2) Rhythmic emphasis on beats 1 and 3.
3) Snare drum on beats 2 and 4.

Ex. 6

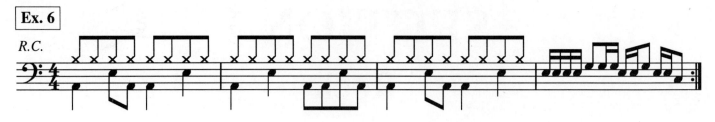

Ex. 7

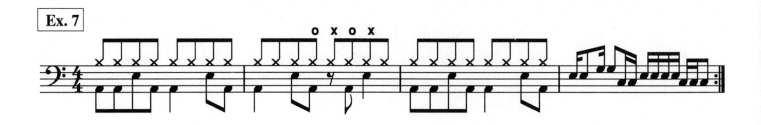

Ex. 8

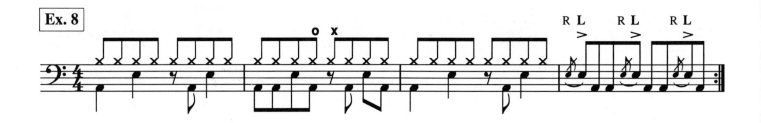

This pattern uses an introduction fill. Such fills are used to introduce a song and are not played when repeat signs are taken.

Ex. 9

Ex. 10

Ex. 11

Examples 36 – 40 show various ways of incorporating tom toms into a rock beat.

Examples 41 – 45 are Funky Rock beats containing more advanced hi-hat/cowbell rhythms.

Ex. 41

Ex. 42

Ex. 43

Ex. 44

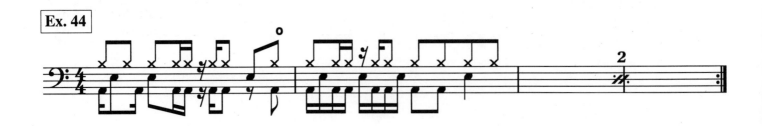

Ex. 45

Thirty second notes are incorporated into snare or bass drum parts in Examples 46 – 50.

Sixteenth note triplets are incorporated into snare and/or bass drum parts in Examples 51–55. Keeping a sixteenth note triplet pulse constantly running in your head can help you with the feel of these examples.

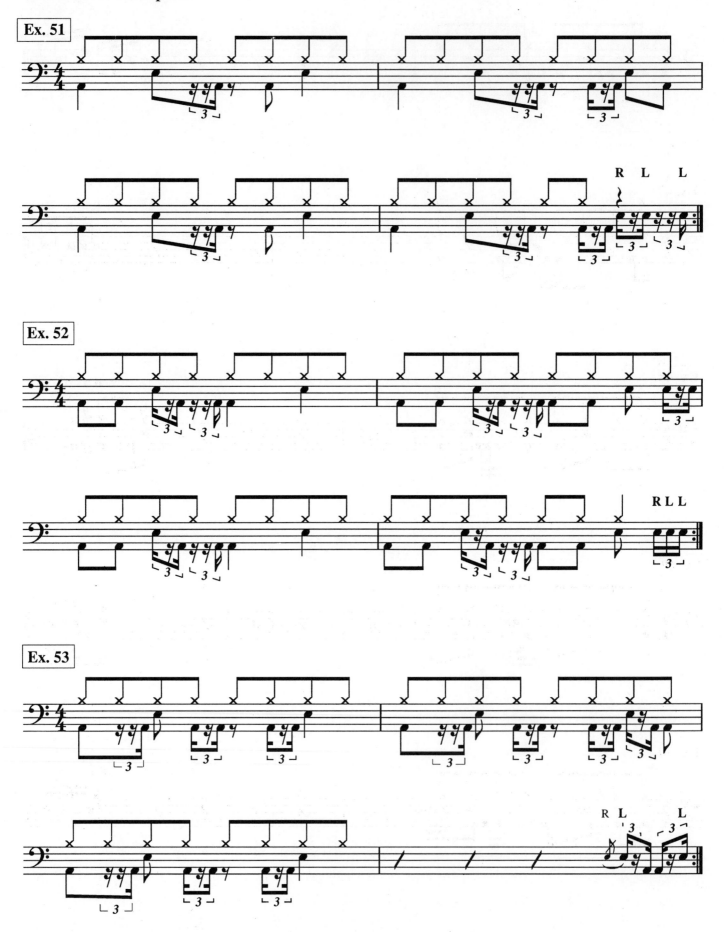

Ex. 54

Ex. 55

SECTION 2
Shuffle and Blues

The term Shuffle refers to the triplet pattern as illustrated in the hi-hat part of Example 56. Shuffle grooves are also categorised by their use of a strong backbeat (beats 2 and 4). The term Blues refers to music which relies harmonically upon the blues scale.

Ex. 69

Ex. 70

Ex. 71

Ex. 72

Ex. 73

Ex. 74

Ex. 75

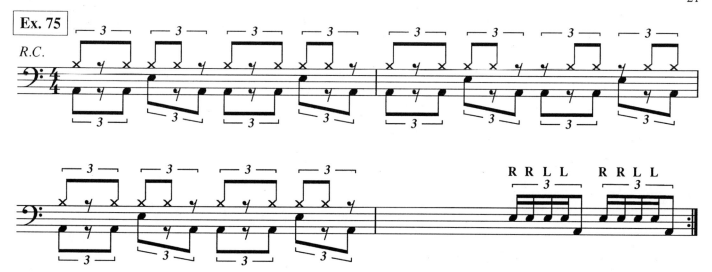

A constant triplet pulse played on hi-hat or ride cymbal is typical of slower blues tunes and ballads. Examples 76 – 80 all contain a right hand triplet pulse.

Sixteenth note triplets can be used effectively in hi-hat, snare or bass drum parts, as examples 81 – 90 illustrate.

SECTION 3
Heavy Metal

This style relies heavily upon sound production and distorted guitar sounds and possesses many similarities to Rock.

26

This pattern has the left hand playing a buzz stroke in beat 4 (listen to the recording). The length of the buzz stroke is a matter of personal choice.

SECTION 4
Reggae

The Reggae style originated in Jamaica and is characterised by its use of rhythmic emphasis on beats 2, 3 and 4.

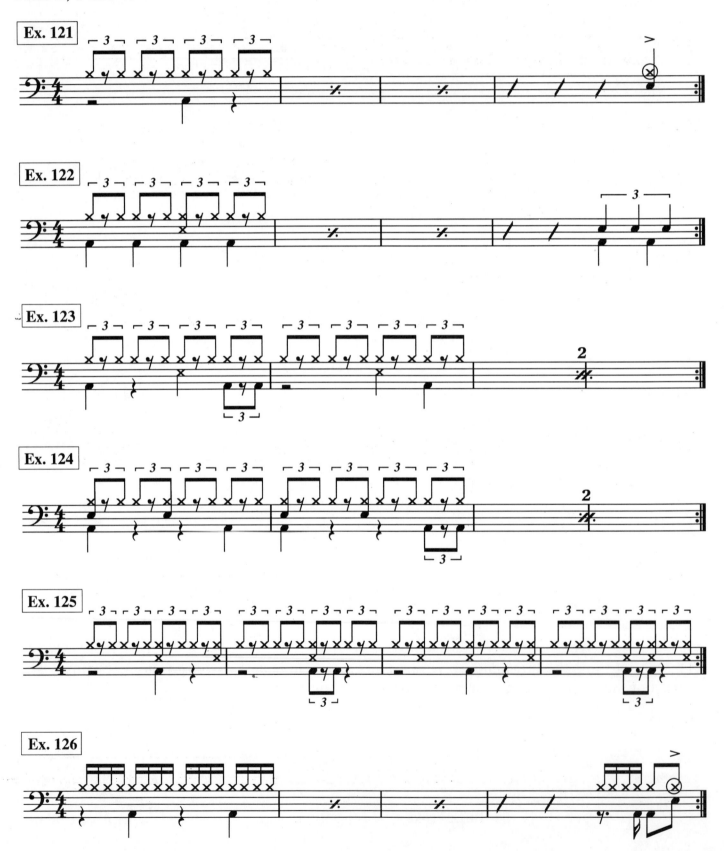

A combination of normal snare and side-stick is used in this example.

Ex. 138

Ex. 139

Ex. 140

Ex. 141

Ex. 142

Ex. 143

This pattern uses a similar technique to Example 135. The left hand alternates between normal snare and side-stick.

SECTION 5
Rap

Rap music has the following features:

1) Relies heavily upon sampling
2) Generally beats one and three are accented
3) Uses syncopation and anticipation
4) Possesses similarities to Funk and Rock

Note: Unless otherwise indicated, use a single stroke sticking (RLRL etc.) between the hi-hat and snare parts.

Ex. 151

Ex. 152

Ex. 153

Ex. 154

Ex. 155

Ex. 156

In this pattern, the right hand alternates between the hi-hat and the ride cymbal bell.

SECTION 6
Go-Go / Hip Hop

The Go-Go style uses a triplet or 'swung' feel and draws upon aspects of Funk/Fusion, Rock and Rap.

Note: Go-Go/Hip-Hop beats are normally played as sixteenth note triplets. However, for ease of reading, they are written here as eighth note triplets.

Ex. 207

Ex. 208

SECTION 7
Funk/Fusion

The style of Funk/Fusion possesses similarities to Rock, but has more common usage of 'staccato feels', syncopation and anticipation, and more complex rhythmic and harmonic ideas.

Examples 229 to 233 use more complex variations of a technique used in Example 177.
Incorporating both hi-hat and ride cymbal bell into a pattern creates a lot of rhythmic interest
and 'forward motion'.

SECTION 8
Latin

Latin music is the broad term used to categorise a large number of individual regional styles from Latin America. Within each of these styles exists a large number of different drum patterns and possibilities. Therefore, many of the styles covered in this section have more than one example notated. Latin American grooves generally use straight eighth notes and contain very syncopated rhythms and a strong emphasis of offbeats.

Beguine

Cha-Cha

Ex. 236 (includes a fill in bar 4)

Calypso

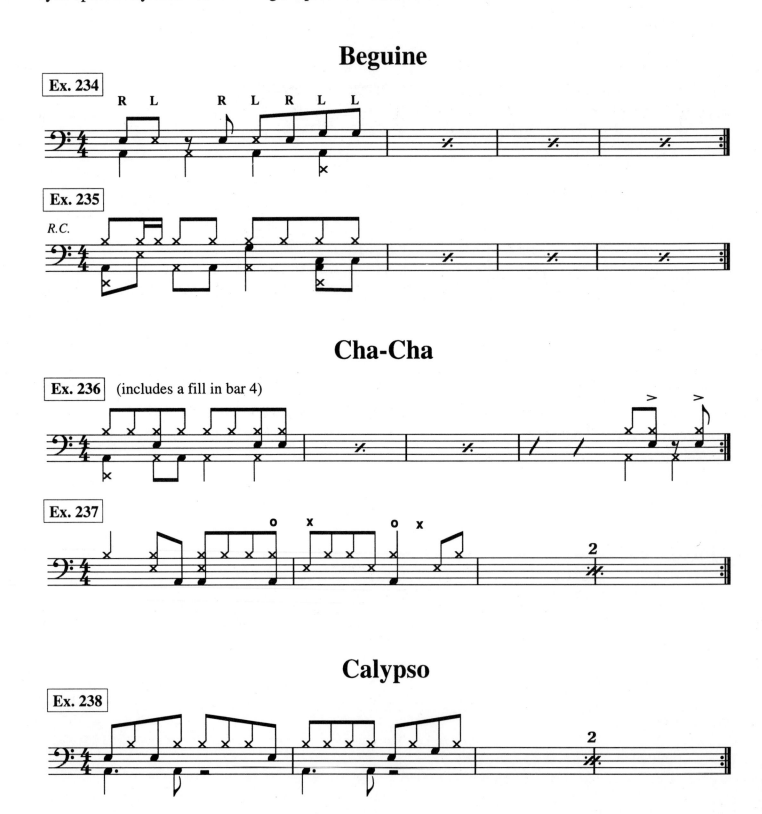

Ex. 239

Bossa Nova

Ex. 240

Fast Bossa Nova

Ex. 241

Mambo

Ex. 242 (includes a fill in bar 4)

Ex. 243

Fast Mambo

Ex. 244 (includes a fill in bar 4)

Rhumba

Ex. 245

Songo

Ex. 246

Ex. 247

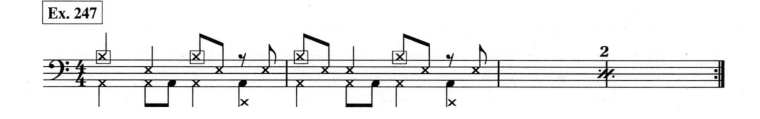

Samba

Ex. 248 (includes a fill in bar 4)

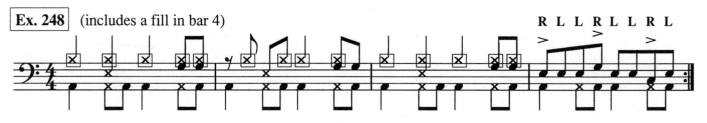

Ex. 249 (includes a fill in bar 4)

Mozambique

Ex. 250 (includes a 2 bar fill in bars 3 and 4)

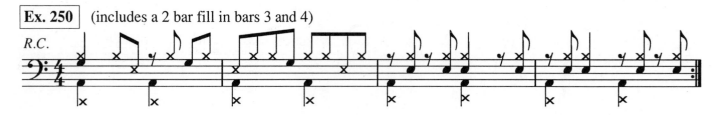

Guaguanco

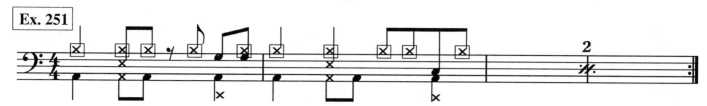

Pagode

Baiao

Afro-Cuban

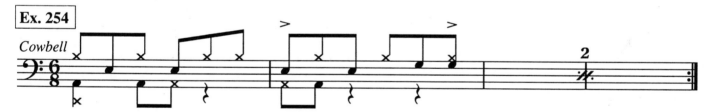

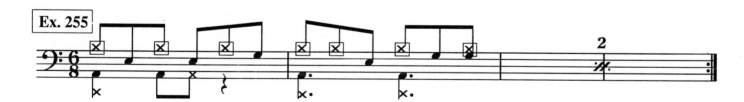

Bembe

Naningo

Ex. 257

Rock Naningo

Ex. 258

SECTION 9
Swing

Swing refers to the predominant ride cymbal pattern used in many Jazz tunes. Example 259 illustrates this ride cymbal pattern.

Ex. 265

Ex. 266

Ex. 267

Ex. 268

Ex. 269

Ex. 277

Fast Swing ♩ = 220

Ex. 278

Slow Swing ♩ = 112

Ex. 279

Jazz 'Two Feel'

Ex. 280

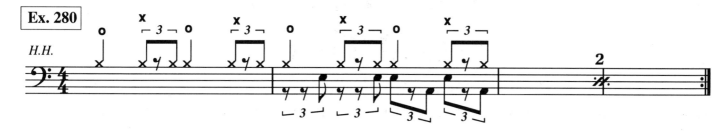

Jazz 'Two Feel'

using the Ride Cymbal

Ex. 281

Jazz 'Two Feel'

with more advanced openings for the Hi-Hat   L   R L R R L L R   R

Ex. 282

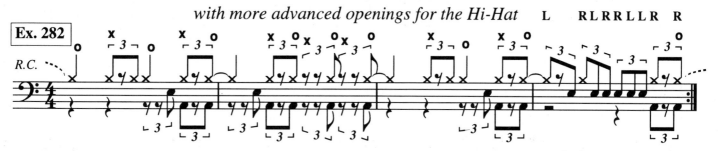

Ex. 283

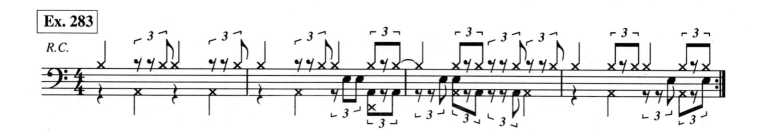

This pattern syncopates the left foot on the hi-hat.

Ex. 284

SECTION 10
Odd Time

Odd Time refers to a bar of music whose time signature has an odd number in the numerator (top number).

Examples 285 – 288 are rock patterns in $\frac{3}{4}$ time.

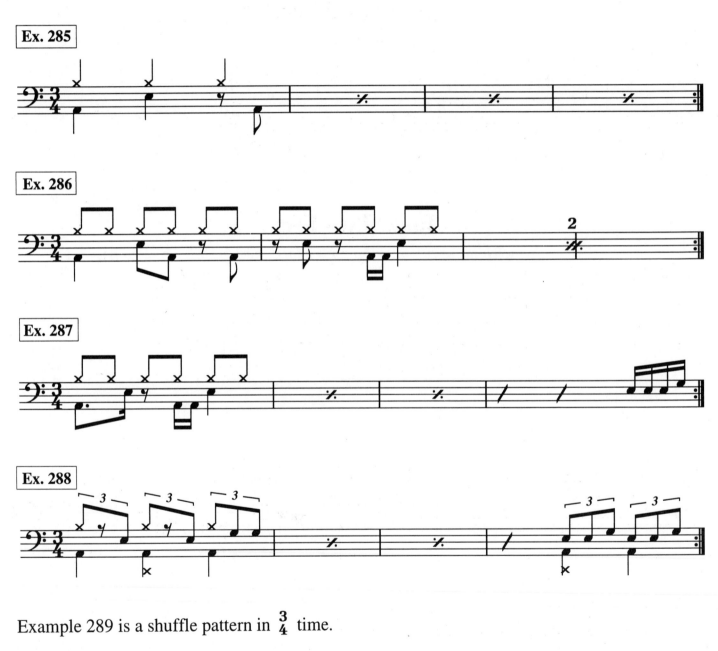

Example 289 is a shuffle pattern in $\frac{3}{4}$ time.

Examples 290 and 291 are funk patterns in $\frac{3}{4}$ time.

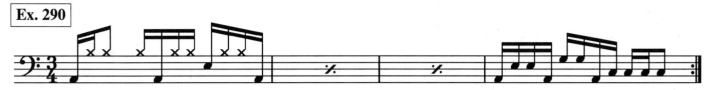

Below is an example of a $\frac{3}{4}$ Latin beat.

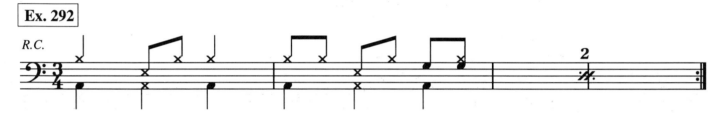

Examples 293 and 294 are swing patterns in $\frac{3}{4}$ time.

This example is a simple $\frac{5}{4}$ rock pattern.

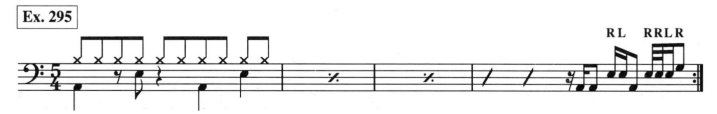

Below is a funky $\frac{5}{4}$ beat.

This is a Latin style $\frac{5}{4}$ pattern.

Examples 298 and 299 are swing patterns in $\frac{5}{4}$ time.

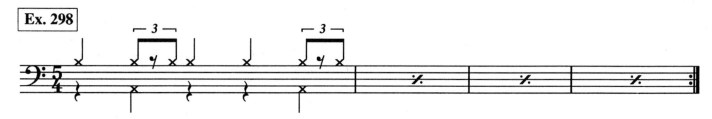

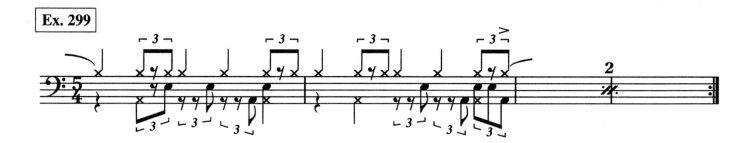

Examples 300 and 301 are funky rock beats in $\frac{7}{4}$ time.

This is a funk pattern in $\frac{7}{4}$ time.

This Latin groove in $\frac{7}{4}$ time uses a complex hi-hat and bass drum rhythm.

Below is an example of a swing beat in $\frac{7}{4}$ time.

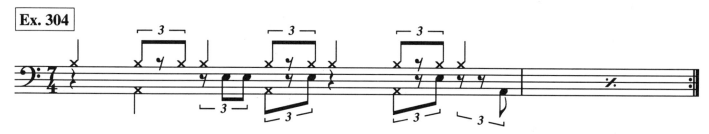

This is an example of a rock groove in $\frac{7}{8}$ time.

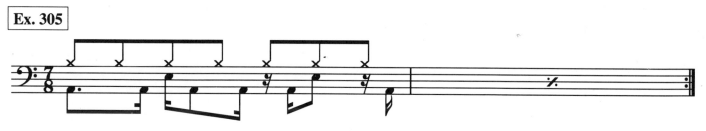

Below is a funk pattern in $\frac{9}{8}$ time.

This $\frac{11}{8}$ groove was used in an interlude section of a Techno Rap song.

Often only one odd time bar will occur within a phrase or section of music.

Below is a two bar rock pattern, the second bar being in $\frac{5}{4}$ time.

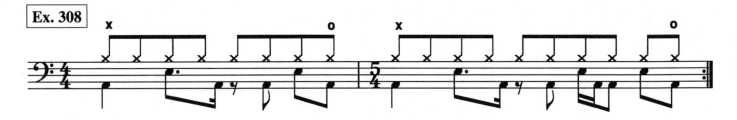